All about

SHIPS

Amazing maritime facts

CHRIS OXLADE

CONSULTANT – TREVOR BLAKELEY

southwater

This edition published by Southwater

Distributed in the UK by The Manning Partnership,
251-253 London Road East, Batheaston, Bath BA1 7RL, UK
tel. (0044) 01225 852 727
fax. (0044) 01225 852 852

Distributed in the USA by Ottenheimer Publishing
5 Park Center Court, Suite 300
Owing Mills MD 2117-5001, USA
tel. (001) 410 902 9100
fax. (001) 410 902 7210

Distributed in Australia by Sandstone Publishing
Unit 1, 360 Norton Street, Leichhardt
New South Wales 2040, Australia
tel. (0061) 2 9560 7888
fax. (0061) 2 9560 7488

Distributed in New Zealand by Five Mile Press NZ
PO Box 33-1071
Takapuna, Auckland 9, New Zealand
tel. (0064) 9 486 1925
fax. (0064) 9 486 1454

Southwater is an imprint of
Anness Publishing Limited
© 1999, 2000 Anness Publishing Limited

10 9 8 7 6 5 4 3 2 1

Printed and bound in Hong Kong

Publisher: Joanna Lorenz
Managing Editor, Children's Books: Gilly Cameron-Cooper
Editor: Charlotte Hurdman
Photographer: John Freeman
Stylist: Melanie Williams
Designer: Caroline Grimshaw
Picture Researcher: Annabel Ossel
Illustrator: Peter Bull Art Studio
Production Controller: Don Campaniello

The publishers would like to thank the following
children, and their parents, for modelling in this book –
Mohammed Afsar, Anthony Bainbridge, Amaru Fleary, Ricky
Garrett, Africa George, Francesca Hill, Carl Keating, Mai Peterson,
Susy Quirke, Kirsty Wells.

All about

SHIPS

Amazing maritime facts

CONTENTS

WHAT IS A SHIP?

PEOPLE have used rafts, boats and ships to travel across water for many thousands of years. At its simplest, a ship is any craft that travels on water, but ships have developed from simple log rafts to vast oil tankers. This development has affected life on land, in shipbuilding yards and at ports where hundreds of people work loading and unloading cargo. The difference between a ship and a boat is not very clear. Generally, ships are larger and travel across seas and oceans. Boats are smaller and usually travel on rivers, lakes and coastal waters. Ships and boats come in a huge variety of shapes and sizes and have a wide range of uses from simple rowing boats to massive cruise liners. The selection of ships and boats shown here illustrates the wide range of jobs they do, and their importance for transport, commerce, leisure, exploration and combat. Simple projects will help you understand the technical side of ships – how they float and how they are powered and controlled.

Boats on inland waters
Two types of boat common on rivers and canals are shown here. In the foreground is a very simple rowing boat. It has many uses – transport, fishing and ferrying from ship to shore. It is usually propelled by oars, but it can be fitted with sails or an outboard motor. Behind is a narrow, flat-bottomed canal boat. It is used for transporting cargo.

Parts of a ship
This fishing trawler looks similar to many other ships and boats. The body of the boat is called the hull. The backbone of the hull is the keel. The bow (front) is sharply pointed to cut easily through the water. A deck provides a watertight covering for the crew to work on. An engine-driven propeller pushes the ship along. The rudder at the stern (back) is used for steering.

Mainmast

Funnel

Mizzen mast (back mast)

Stern

Deck

Bridge

Lifeboat

Bow

Hull

Keel

Propeller

Rudder

Fishing boats

One of the earliest uses of boats was fishing. Today there are fishing boats designed to catch different fish in all sorts of conditions – from calm lakes to the deep oceans. Fishing trawlers drag nets through the water behind them.

Cargo carriers

The largest moving machines ever built are big cargo ships. There are several types designed to carry different types of cargoes. The one pictured here is a container ship, which carries different cargoes packed in large metal boxes.

Fast and fun

The fastest boats are racing powerboats. They are just one of many different types of boats used for having fun on the water. Their hulls are designed to rise out of the water and skim the surface at high speed. The deep V-shape of the hull helps the bow to lift clear of the water and slice through the waves.

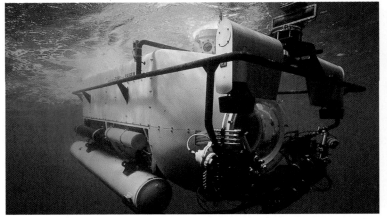

Under the water

Submersibles and submarines are the only types of boat designed to travel under the water as well as on top. The submersible shown here is just breaking the surface of the water. Submersibles are small craft used for underwater research, exploration and repairs to seabed pipes and cables. Submarines are usually larger and most are for military purposes. They are used to launch missiles and sink ships. Most submersibles can dive much deeper than a military submarine.

HOW DO SHIPS FLOAT?

Sʜɪᴘs and all other objects that float can do so because the water they are floating in pushes upwards against them. This pushing force is called upthrust. An object will float if the upthrust of the water is great enough to overcome the downwards push of the object's weight. The size of the upthrust depends on how much water the object pushes out of the way. When you put an object in water and let it go, it settles into the water, pushing liquid out of the way. The farther it goes in, the more water it pushes away and the more upthrust acts on it. When the upthrust becomes the same as the object's weight, the object floats. If, when the object is fully underwater, its weight is bigger than the upthrust, however, it will sink. The simplest boats, such as rafts, float because the material they are made of is less dense (lighter) than water. Heavy metal ships float, because they are specially designed to displace (push aside) a large weight of water. Not all water has the same density. Salt water is denser than fresh water and gives a stronger upthrust. Ships float higher in salty seawater than in fresh lake water.

Fresh water *Salt water*

Measuring density
The density of water is measured with a hydrometer. Make a simple hydrometer by putting a lump of modelling clay on the end of a straw. Put it in a glass of water and mark the water level with tape. Now put the straw in an equal amount of salty water. What happens?

TESTING UPTHRUST

You will need: two polystyrene blocks (one twice the size of the other), wooden block, marble.

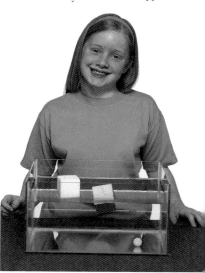

1 Put the two polystyrene blocks into a tank of water. They will float well, because their material, polystyrene, is so light. Only a small amount of upthrust is needed.

2 Try pushing the blocks under the water. Now you are pushing lots of water aside. Can you feel upthrust pushing back? The bigger block will experience more upthrust.

3 A wooden block floats deeper in the water, because wood is more dense (heavier) than polystyrene. A marble sinks, because the upthrust on it is not as great as its weight.

HOLLOW HULLS

You will need: scissors, aluminium foil, ruler, marbles.

1 Put a piece of aluminium foil about 20cm by 15cm into a tank of water. It will sink. This is because it does not displace much water so there is very little upthrust.

2 Lift the sheet of foil out of the water. Now mould it into a simple boat shape with your fingers. Take care not to tear the foil.

3 Put your foil boat back into the tank of water. It should now float. Its shape pushes aside much more water than it did when it was flat, so the upthrust is greater.

4 Try filling your foil boat with small objects such as marbles, for cargo. As you put more marbles in it will float lower and lower. How many marbles can your boat hold before it sinks?

The boat shape traps air inside it and pushes aside more water.

Foil float

This simple foil boat works like a real ship's hull. Even though it is made of metal, it is filled with air. This gives the hull shape a much lower overall density.

THE FIRST BOATS

NOBODY knows exactly when people first started using craft to travel on water, but it must have been tens of thousands of years ago. The first craft were probably extremely simple – perhaps just a log, an inflated animal skin, or a bundle of reeds tied together. People discovered that craft like these, made from what was available close by, could help them to cross a stretch of water more easily. These craft probably developed into early simple boats, such as dug-out canoes and skin-covered boats, in which a person could sit while fishing or travelling along a river. The basic designs are still in use in many areas of the world today and have many advantages over modern boats. They are simple to make from cheap local materials. Although they are not very long-lasting, there are no high-tech materials to mend or engine parts to replace. The simplest boats do not use up expensive fuel or hard-to-find equipment such as batteries.

Simple raft
A raft like this one from Australia can be built with very basic tools. It is used in shallow water and propelled along with a long stick pushed into the riverbed. Rafts are probably the oldest form of water transport. Aboriginals may have used sea-going rafts to first reach Australia around 55,000 years ago.

Dug-out canoe
A dug-out canoe is made by hollowing out a thick tree trunk to leave a thin wooden hull. The hull is smoothed and shaped so that it moves easily through the water. Dug-out canoes are fairly heavy boats and sit low in the water.

Yak-skin boat
This strange-looking boat was photographed on a river in Tibet, now part of China. It is made by stretching yak hides (a type of ox skin) over a wooden framework. The hide is then treated to make it waterproof.

FACT BOX

• In 1970, Norwegian Thor Heyerdahl built a large Egyptian-style reed boat called *Ra II*. He sailed it from Africa to the Caribbean. This proved the Egyptians would have been able to reach America more than 4,000 years ago.

• One of the greatest sea battles of all time took place at Salamis, off Greece, in 480BC. In the battle, 380 Greek triremes defeated an invading fleet of around 1,000 Persian ships.

Inuit kayak

The kayak was developed by the Inuit people of the Arctic. It is also a hide boat, made from sealskin stretched over a driftwood frame. Kayaks were used as fast hunting craft for harpooning seals, fish and walruses. Boats like this work well in rough seas. A skilled paddler can turn the kayak upright if it capsizes (rolls over).

Nile boat

A model boat from an ancient Egyptian tomb shows the type of craft used on the river Nile about 5,000 years ago. Boats like these were the first to use a simple sail. The boat was propelled with oars when there was no wind or the wind was in the wrong direction. It was steered using a long oar hanging over the stern.

Square sail

A tiller (handle) was used to move the steering oar.

Steering oar

Rigging (ropes and poles)

The helmsman steered the boat.

A crew raised and lowered the mast, or rowed the boat.

Shallow-scooped, wooden hull

Oar *Passenger*

Greek warship

This is a full-scale replica of an ancient Greek trireme. A trireme was a warship with three banks of oars operated by about 170 men. Triremes attacked other ships by ramming them. Soldiers were also transported on deck.

Roman galley

A Roman mosaic from Tunisia, made around AD200, shows that Roman warships were very similar to earlier Greek ships. In the stern they often had wooden towers painted to look like stone. Underneath the high bow was a ram.

MAKE SIMPLE BOATS

You can build your own models of ancient types of boat that are still in use today. Instructions for making a model reed boat are given in the first project. Reed boats are made by tying thousands of river reeds together into huge bundles. The bundles themselves are then tied together to make hull shapes. Small reed boats are still built in southern Iraq and on Lake Titicaca in South America. In ancient Egypt, quite large boats were made like this from papyrus reeds. Some historians believe that Egyptians may have made long ocean crossings in papyrus craft. The model in the second project is of a craft called a coracle. This is a round boat made by covering a light wooden frame with animal hides. Like reed boats, coracles are still made, but today builders use a covering of canvas treated with tar instead of hide. They were small enough for one person to paddle along a river and were used for fishing. Look for pictures of other simple craft and try making working models of them, too.

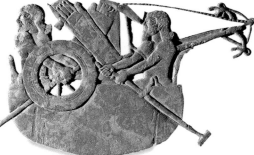

Chariots, boats and bladders
A stone carving from 860BC shows Assyrian soldiers crossing the river Tigris. They are transporting a war chariot in their coracle-like boat. Assyrian soldiers also used inflated pig's bladders as buoyancy aids to help them swim across wide rivers.

MAKE A REED CRAFT

You will need: large bunch of raffia, scissors, ruler.

1 Make bundles of raffia by tying a few dozen strands together with a short length of raffia. You will need two bundles about 20cm long and two more about 25cm long.

2 Tie the two long bundles and the two short bundles together. Tie the short bundles on top of the long ones. Fix a strand between each end to make the ends bend up.

3 Gently lower the reed boat on to the surface of a tank of water. How well does it float? Does it stay upright? Try leaving it in the water to see if it becomes waterlogged.

MAKE A CORACLE

You will need: scissors, craft cane, string, dark cotton cloth, PVA glue, paint brush.

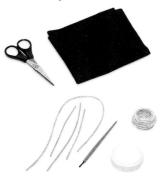

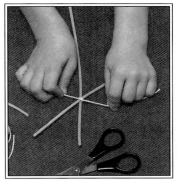

1 Cut one long and three short pieces of cane. Using short lengths of string, tie all three short pieces to the long piece to make a triple-armed cross.

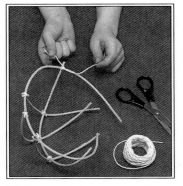

2 Cut a much longer piece of cane. Form it into a loop and tie it to all the ends of the triple cross shape. Bend the ends of the cross up as you tie them to form a dish shape.

Waterproof covering

Lightweight frame

Model of an ancient craft
The design of the coracle has not changed in thousands of years. Early Britons used them 9,000 years ago. They are light to carry, easy to manoeuvre and stable enough to fish from.

3 Cut pieces of cotton cloth about 15cm by 5cm. Apply glue to the outside of the frame and put the pieces over it. Glue the pieces to each other where they overlap.

4 Glue down the cloth where it folds over the top of the frame. Put two coats of glue on the outside of the cloth to waterproof it. Leave the glue to dry completely.

5 When dry, put the finished coracle into a tank of water. How well does it float? Why not try making a person from modelling clay to sit in your model coracle?

THE AGE OF SAIL

S AILS capture the wind and use it to push ships and boats along. As far as experts can tell, sails first appeared on ships on the river Nile in about 3500BC. These ships had just one simple square sail on a single mast. They were only useful when the wind was blowing in the same direction that the crew of the ship wanted to go. If the wind was blowing in another direction, such as from their destination, the crew had to row there instead. Viking boats in the AD600s used square sails to sail the coasts of Scandinavia. Later, large coastal Viking ships crossed the Atlantic to reach North America. In the Middle Ages, the lateen (triangular) sail was invented by the Chinese and Arabs. The lateen sail allowed ships to be sailed with the wind from the side. From the 1100s, European sailors began building fully-rigged ships with a combination of square and lateen sails. This allowed them to make the maximum use of the wind. Their boats also had sturdy, seaworthy hulls. In ships like these, European sailors began long voyages of exploration.

Viking sails
A stone carving from Sweden that dates from the AD700s shows a Viking merchant boat with a simple square sail. The sail was made from cloth reinforced with diagonal strips of leather. Sails like this helped the crew sail downwind.

Chinese way ahead
The Chinese developed multi-masted ships called junks. These used triangular sails several centuries before they were introduced to Europe. This modern junk has sails that hang from poles that are hauled up the mast. The sails can swivel around the mast to take advantage of wind from behind or the side. They are made with cloth stiffened by bamboo poles. The poles keep the sails flat, make it easy to fold up the sails and provide a handy ladder for the crew.

Triangular sails
This fishing boat on the river Nile is called a felucca. Its design has been in use for 1,000 years and is most often seen on Arab trading vessels called dhows. The single triangular sail is an example of a lateen sail.

A mixture of sails
This painting shows ships off the coast of
Portugal in the 1520s. The large ships are
heavily-armed carracks, a design that used
both square and triangular sails. Smaller
carracks were used as merchant vessels.
The flagship *Santa Maria*, which took
Columbus to America in 1492, was
probably a small carrack.

Men-of-war
These French
ships are typical
of the men-of-
war (warships)
that developed by
1700. They had
many rows of
cannons and
hulls that were
richly carved
and gilded.

Life onboard
A cartoon shows sailors celebrating victory in battle
with Admiral Nelson in 1798. Hundreds of men
were needed to sail a man-of-war. They lived in
cramped conditions on the gun decks. Tables and
hammocks were suspended between the guns.

The golden age of sail
By the 1850s, sleek, fast and efficient ships called clippers carried
cargo such as tea and wool around the world. They represented
the peak of sailing ship design and were the largest wooden vessels
ever built. Larger merchant ships with iron hulls and up to seven
masts were built up to the 1930s.

STEAM POWER

THE first steam engines were developed in the early 1700s for pumping water out of mines. By the end of the century they had become small and more efficient and engineers began to use them in trains and ships. Steam power meant that a ship could keep going even if the wind was in the wrong direction, or not blowing at all. The first craft to use steam power was a small river boat called the *Charlotte Dundas*, launched in 1802. At sea, steamships carried sails to save fuel when the wind was blowing in the right direction. Early steamships used paddles, but propellers gradually proved to be more efficient. After the 1850s, shipbuilders began to use iron instead of wood. The superior strength of iron meant that much larger ships could be built, which could also be fitted with more powerful steam engines.

Stoking the boilers
To create steam, stokers constantly fed the fire boxes under a ship's boilers with coal. It was hot, unpleasant work in the stokehole.

Crossing the Atlantic
The huge *Great Eastern* was built in 1858. Steamships arrived at a time when crossing the Atlantic Ocean was becoming more popular. Steam power allowed faster and more reliable crossings, which people were willing to pay for. The *Great Eastern* could carry 4,000 passengers. It was the only ship to have both paddles and a propeller. But passengers did not quite trust steam, so it was also fitted with sails.

An iron monster
This print shows the construction of the *Great Eastern's* central compartment. At 210m long and 32,000 tonnes, it was by far the largest ship in the world at its launch in 1858. It was the last of three revolutionary ships designed by British engineer Isambard Kingdom Brunel. The *Great Eastern's* design was copied on other steamships for several decades. The hull was divided into ten watertight compartments, with double iron plating from the keel to the waterline. It took three months and seven attempts to finally launch the *Great Eastern*. Unfortunately, it had a pronounced roll in heavy seas, which passengers did not like. The ship was sold for scrap in 1888.

Paddle-powered riverboats on the Mississippi

On the shallow rivers of the southern USA, steam powered riverboats with huge paddles were developed. Here, two riverboats are racing each other on the Mississippi River in about 1850. Riverboats had flat, shallow hulls and no keel. Paddlewheels were mounted on each side, or at the stern.

Steaming to war

Steam power and iron construction gave warships much greater speed, manoeuvrability and strength. *Dreadnought,* built in 1906, was the fastest battleship of its day and became the model for the period.

Tramp steamer

A typical cargo ship was known as a three-island steamer. This was because it had three raised decks, or islands. They were also called tramp steamers if they sailed from port to port with no fixed route.

Luxury travel

As transatlantic travel grew, shipping companies built large, luxurious ships called liners. This 1920s poster is from the golden age of the liner. Rival companies competed to provide the quickest crossing.

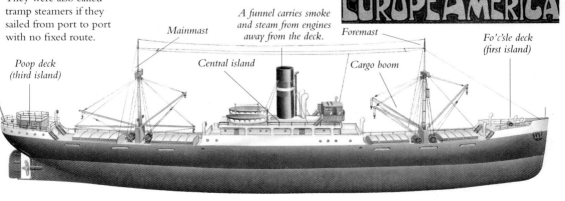

Poop deck (third island)

Mainmast

A funnel carries smoke and steam from engines away from the deck.

Central island

Foremast

Cargo boom

Fo'c'sle deck (first island)

SHIPBUILDING

S HIPS are constructed in a shipbuilding yard. Large ships are usually made from steel. Generally, the hull is built first by welding pieces of steel together. Often the hull is built in large sections that are then welded together. When the hull is finished, the ship is launched on to the water, where the rest of the ship is completed. Dozens of different tradespeople, such as welders, crane drivers, painters, electricians and carpenters work in shipyards. Boatbuilding takes place in smaller boatyards. Boats are usually made from wood or glass-reinforced plastic (GRP).

Shipbuilding methods have changed as new materials have become available. Originally all ships were made from wood. A skeleton hull was made, then covered with planks. Steel ships are built with the metal skin forming part of the structure. New ships are designed on computer and models of them are tested before being built.

Viking boatbuilders
This is part of the Bayeux Tapestry. It shows Norman shipwrights building the fleet that invaded England in 1066. The Normans were descended from the Vikings and shared many of the same boatbuilding techniques. They used special tools, such as axes and augers (hole borers), to shape the hull of a ship. Slender, Viking war boats were called longships.

FACT BOX

• The size of a ship is given in gross registered tonnage (g.r.t.). This is not a measure of its weight, but of the space inside it. One ton is equal to 2.8 cubic metres.

• The displacement of a ship is equal to the weight of the water that it pushes out of the way when it floats. This is usually equal to the weight of the ship and everything on it.

• The deadweight of a ship is the difference between the ship's displacement when empty and when it is full. It measures the weight of the cargo and passengers.

Wooden ribs
Here, the ribs of a wooden boat are being attached to the central keel. The timbers form a skeleton frame to which the planks of the hull and deck will be attached.

Covering the hull
Planks are attached edge to edge to the ribs of a wooden boat to make a smooth hull. The tight-fitting planks will be given several coats of paint or varnish to make a watertight finish.

Naval architects

Just as there are architects who design buildings, there are naval architects who design ships. These architects are planning the deck layouts of the cruise liner *Oriana*.

Shipbuilding shed

This picture shows the bow section of the cruise liner *Oriana* under construction. You can see the steel decks, bulkheads (watertight walls and doors) and skin. The ship is being built in a huge construction shed, where its progress is unaffected by the weather.

Float out

Once the hull has been completed, the floor of the construction shed is flooded so that the entire hull can be floated out. Here *Oriana* is being floated out at its launch. Smaller ships are built on slipways before being launched by sliding them down into the water.

Fitting out

Work on electrical equipment, lighting, pipes and other fixtures and fittings is completed after the ship is launched. This process is called fitting out. After fitting out, the ship will undergo sea trials.

HULLS

THE main part of a ship is the hull, which sits in the water. The hull does four things. It provides the strong, rigid shape that makes the structure of the ship. It is a waterproof skin that stops water getting in. It supports all the equipment in the ship, such as the engines, and it provides space for the cargo. The shape of the hull also lets the ship slide easily through the water. The hull shape of a ship or boat depends on what that ship or boat is designed to do. Long, thin hulls are designed for travelling at speed, while broad hulls are designed to carry as much cargo as possible. Wide, shallow hulls float high in the water and are good for travelling on shallow lakes, rivers and canals. The hull shape also dictates the stability of the ship, or how easily it tips from side to side. Inside the hull, solid walls called bulkheads make the hull stiffer and divide it into a number of watertight compartments.

Hulls for floating
Try pushing a light ball underwater. It will spring back up. Upthrust from the water makes a hollow hull float in the same way.

Multi-hulls
This canoe will not tip over because it has outriggers. The outriggers work like small hulls on each side of the canoe, making it a very stable vessel. Catamarans (boats with two hulls) and trimarans (three hulls) work in the same way. Boats with only one hull are called mono-hulls.

Plastic hulls
A white-water kayak has a one-piece hull made of tough, rigid plastic. Its materials are strong enough to resist bumping against rocks and the riverbed. The hull's long, thin shape is designed for speed, slicing through the rough water. The canoeist sits in a sealed cockpit, which prevents water getting in. This not only keeps the canoeist dry, but means that the kayak remains buoyant (afloat).

Hulls in halves

Here, two halves of a yacht hull are made from GRP (glass-reinforced plastic). GRP is made by filling moulds with layers of glass fibre and glue. It is light but strong and has a smooth finish.

Points and bulbs

While a fishing boat is in dry dock it enables us to see the parts of the hull usually underwater. The bulb shape at the bottom of the bow helps the boat to slip more easily through the water.

Changing shape

If you could cut through a ship and look at the cut ends, you would see a cross-section of its hull. Here you can see how the cross-section of a container ship's hull changes along its length.

Overlapping planks

This is a head-on view of the bow of a 1,000-year-old Viking ship. The hull is made from a shell of overlapping planks, hammered together with nails and strengthened by internal ribs. Hulls constructed of overlapping planks are called clinker built.

Stempost

Ocean-going high bow

Wide, stable hull shape

16 overlapping oak planks

Keel

Stern cross-section
The sides curve inwards to make the bottom narrower than the deck.

Central cross-section
The hull is almost square. This allows the maximum space for cargo.

Bow cross-section
Just behind the sharp bow the bottom is very narrow and the sides are high.

FAST AND SLOW

WHENEVER an object such as a ship moves through the water, the water tries to slow it down. The push that the water makes against the object is called water resistance, or drag. The faster the object moves, the bigger the water resistance gets. If you look around a busy harbour, you will see dozens of different hull designs. Sleek, narrow hulls with sharp bows cause less resistance than wide hulls with square bows, so they can move through the water faster. You can test how the shape of a bow affects the speed of a ship in the project below. The deeper a hull sits in the water, the more resistance there is. Some hulls are designed to just touch the water. For example, a small speedboat has a flaring, V-shaped hull designed to skim across the surface. A cargo ship, however, has a more square-shaped hull that sits lower in the water. Speed is not as important for the cargo ship as it is for the speedboat. Instead, the cargo ship is designed for stability and to carry the maximum amount of cargo.

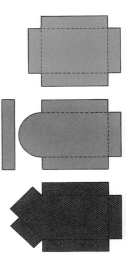

TESTING HULL SHAPES

You will need: coloured stiff card, pen or pencil, ruler, scissors, sticky tape, aluminium foil, paper clips, modelling clay, weighing scales, string, watering can, long plastic tray or trough, three equal wooden bricks.

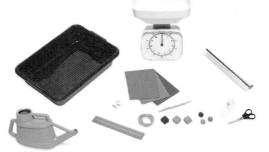

Templates
Use these three templates to help you cut out and make the three boat shapes in this project. Their dimensions are roughly 15cm long, by 10cm wide. Make the sides of each boat shape about 3cm deep.

1 Use a ruler to carefully draw out the three templates shown above on sheets of stiff card. Make sure the corners are square and the edges straight. Cut out the shapes.

2 Using scissors, score along the lines inside the base of each shape (shown as broken lines above). Bend up the sides and use sticky tape to fix the corners together.

3 Make the round-ended and pointed boats in the same way as the first boat. Use a separate piece of card to make the round bow and tape to the base in several places.

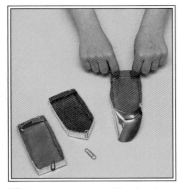

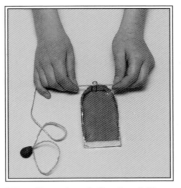

4 Now cover the outside of each shape with foil, neatly folding the foil over the sides. This will make the shapes more waterproof. Fix a paper clip to the bow of each boat.

5 Roll out three balls of modelling clay about the size of a walnut. Weigh the balls to make sure they are the same weight. Attach a ball to the bow of each boat with string.

6 Put a large plastic bowl or long trough on to a table or a strong box. Fill the trough with water to about 1cm from the top of the trough.

Try timing the boats with a stopwatch. You could find the difference between the fastest and slowest.

8 Release the boats all at the same time. The weighted strings will pull them along down the length of the trough. Which one wins the race to the other end of the trough?

7 Line up the boats at one end of the trough. Hang the strings and modelling clay balls down over the other end of the trough. Put a small wooden brick inside each boat.

The shapes on test

Boats' hulls are usually pointed to help them cut through the water. Energy is wasted pushing a flat end through the water, which makes a boat slower.

SHIP POWER

Punting
In a punt, a person stands on the back of the boat to push down on a long pole against the bottom of the river. Each push propels the boat forwards. The pole is also used to steer the punt and keep it straight.

THERE are many different ways of propelling boats and ships through the water. The most basic, such as rowing and paddling, are human-powered. Oars and paddles work by pushing against the water. Today, they are only used in small vessels. Sails harness the natural power of the wind to propel a boat or ship. Engines convert the energy stored in fuel into the movement of a propeller. As the propeller spins, its blades force water to rush backwards, which thrusts the boat or ship forwards. Most engines used in boats and ships are diesel engines. Other types of marine engine are petrol engines, gas turbine engines and steam turbine engines. Some short-distance ferries move by pulling themselves along a wire or chain attached to the bank on the other side of a lake or river. Other craft, such as hovercraft, have aircraft-like propellers. These are useful in very shallow or plant-filled water where an underwater propeller could be easily damaged.

FACT BOX

• In 1845, two ships, one with a propeller and one with paddlewheels, fought a tug-of-war. The battle was to find the most efficient. The propeller easily won.

• In future boats may lift up out of the water altogether. Wingships use air pressure to skim above the water's surface. They can fly along about 2m above the waves.

• In the swamps of Southern USA, people travel in swamp skimmers pushed along by a huge fan at the back.

Rowing with oars
An oar is a long pole with a flattened blade at one end. It is fixed to a pivot on the edge of the rowboat, called a rowlock. The rower faces backwards and propels the boat forwards with a continuous cycle of strokes. Rowing a boat using a pair of oars is called sculling.

Paddles
A dragon boat from Hong Kong is propelled along by a team of paddlers. A paddle is a short pole with a flat blade at one end used to propel a canoe. Paddles are easier to manoeuvre than oars, but they are not as efficient.

Propeller power

A propeller is made up of several angled blades (usually between two and six) attached to a central hub. The enormous propeller being checked here will be one of a pair used on a large cruise liner. Its blades are specially curved to cut down turbulence as water is drawn past the hull. Each propeller will be driven by an electric motor.

Pits on the surface of the blades help with water flow.

Capturing the wind

Sails catch the wind and push a boat along. The sailors adjust the position of their sails to make the best use of the wind. These yachts have the wind blowing from behind and are using large sails called spinnakers for extra speed.

Housing for petrol engine

Throttle (controls speed)

Clamp

Driveshaft

Propeller

Portable power

An outboard motor is a self-contained portable power unit for small boats. It is attached to the stern of the boat by a strong clamp. A petrol engine at the top drives the propeller via a driveshaft. Twisting the throttle controls the speed of the propeller. Moving it from side to side changes the direction of the boat. When not in use, the whole engine can be unclamped and taken away.

Jet propulsion

A jet ski has no propeller. Instead, its engine sucks in water and pumps it out of the back of the ski in a powerful jet. The jet of water shooting out backwards pushes the ski forwards. Boats powered by waterjets can reach much higher speeds with less wear and tear than those with propellers.

CONTROLLING A SHIP

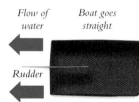

ALL ships and boats have simple controls for steering. Usually this is a rudder at the stern. The rudder is controlled by a tiller (handle) or wheel. The rudder only works when the boat or ship is moving through the water. Powered craft also have engine controls for adjusting speed. Many boats have twin propellers and can also be steered by running the engines at different speeds or in different directions (forwards or reverse). Large ships may also have bow and stern thrusters, which are used in port to push the ship sideways or rotate it on the spot. On modern cruise liners, which often have to enter a different dock every night of the cruise, the ship can be moved by means of a small joystick on the bridge. Large modern ships have a computerized autopilot like that on an aircraft. This automatically adjusts the rudder and engine speed to follow a set course.

Simple rudder
The rudder on a Norman ship from the Bayeux Tapestry is a single oar. The long oar is set on the right side of the ship at the stern. Many early boats were steered with simple side rudders like this.

Flow of water   *Boat goes straight*

Rudder

How a rudder works
The rudder works by cutting into the flow of water. With the rudder in the centre, water flows past each side and the boat goes in a straight line.

Flow of water is deflected left

Rudder is turned to left

When the rudder is turned to the side, the flow of water is deflected away to that side.

Boat turns to the left

The water pushes hard against the blade of the rudder. This makes the stern go to the right, swinging the bow left.

Boat travels ahead

Rudder straight

When enough turn has been made, the rudder is brought back to the centre. The boat straightens out and travels ahead on its new course.

Under the stern
Here, the propeller and rudder of a cargo ship are being cleaned of barnacles in dry dock. In almost all ships and boats, the rudder is fixed behind the propeller under the stern. The rudder is turned by machinery in the stern that is controlled from the bridge. The propeller pushes water past the rudder, which makes the ship easier to turn from side to side at slow speed.

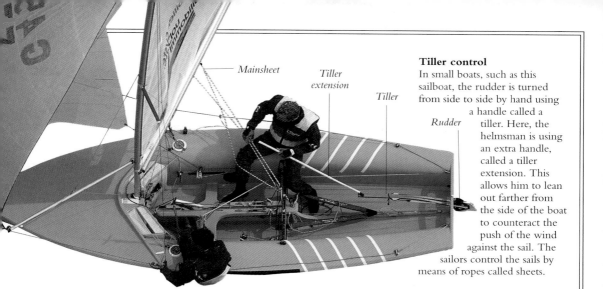

Mainsheet

Tiller
extension

Tiller

Rudder

Tiller control

In small boats, such as this sailboat, the rudder is turned from side to side by hand using a handle called a tiller. Here, the helmsman is using an extra handle, called a tiller extension. This allows him to lean out farther from the side of the boat to counteract the push of the wind against the sail. The sailors control the sails by means of ropes called sheets.

On the bridge

The bridge (also sometimes called the wheelhouse) is the control centre of a ship. There are rudder and engine controls and navigation equipment, such as a compass and radar. The bridge is high up on the ship to give good, all-round visibility.

Steering wheel

On larger yachts a tiller would be too cumbersome to use. Instead, the rudder is operated by a large wheel linked to the rudder by a system of pulleys. The helmsman steers the yacht from the cockpit.

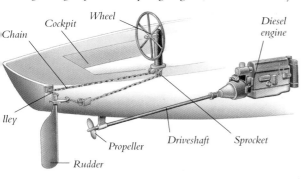

Chain

Cockpit

Wheel

Diesel
engine

lley

Propeller

Driveshaft

Sprocket

Rudder

Connecting up the wheel and the propeller

In this large cruise yacht, the rudder is moved by wires linked to the wheel in the cockpit. The wheel drives a sprocket, which moves a chain. Wires attached to the chain move the rudder via a set of pulleys. The yacht is also equipped with a diesel engine that is connected to a single propeller via a driveshaft. A soundproof engine room insulates the hull from noise and vibration made by the engine.

POWER AND STEERING

THE project below will show you how to build a simple boat driven by a propeller and controlled by a rudder. The propeller is powered by the energy stored in a wound-up elastic band. The two blades of the propeller are set at different angles and push the water backwards as the propeller spins. In turn, this makes the boat move forwards. When you have built your model, you could try making other designs of propeller (for example more blades set at different angles) and testing them to see which works best. After making the propeller you can add a rudder. The rudder can be moved to different positions to make your model boat turn to the left or right, but it will only work when the boat is moving along. Without the rudder, the boat does not go in a straight line very well. So, as well as making the boat turn from side to side, the rudder also helps your model (as it does a full-size boat) travel straight ahead.

Simple propeller
The simplest propeller has two blades that twist in opposite directions. This is the propeller of a small pleasure boat. Three- and four-bladed propellers are more powerful. The hole in the centre is where the driveshaft from the engine fits into the propeller.

MAKE A POWERED BOAT

You will need: cork, bradawl, scissors, small plastic bottle, large plastic bottle, large paper clip, ruler, pliers, bead, long elastic bands, small pencil, thin garden cane.

1 Make a hole through the middle of the cork using a bradawl. Cut a diagonal slot in either side of the cork. Push two strips of plastic cut from a small bottle into the slots.

2 Cut an oblong strip from one side of the large plastic bottle. This slot is the top of your boat. With the bradawl, make a small hole at the back of your bottle in the bottom.

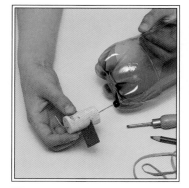

3 Straighten a large paper clip (you may need pliers). Bend the last 1.5cm of wire at right angles. Push the wire through the cork and thread it through the bead and small hole.

The model will go in circles.

4 Bend over the end of the wire inside the bottle. Hook an elastic band over the wire and stretch it up through the neck of the bottle. Secure in place with a pencil.

5 To wind up the band, turn the pencil as you hold on to the propeller. Keep holding the propeller until you put the boat into the water and release it. What happens?

6 Now make a rudder for your boat. Cut a piece of plastic about 4cm by 4cm and pierce two holes near one edge. Push thin cane through the two holes.

Straight and turning
This is the finished model of the boat. To test the controls, start with the rudder centred to make the boat go straight. How tight a circle can you make your boat turn in?

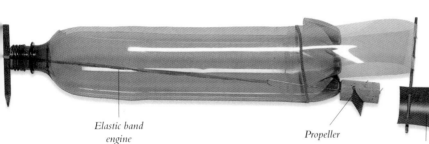

Elastic band engine

Propeller

Rudder

8 Fix the rudder support to the bottle with an elastic band so that the rudder is clear of the propeller. Wind up the elastic band and put your boat back in the water. Try turning the rudder from side to side. What happens?

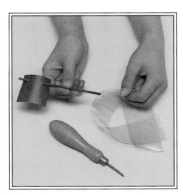

7 Use the strip of plastic cut from the large bottle to support your rudder. Pierce two holes about 2cm apart in the centre of the strip and push the cane through them.

CARGO SHIPS

CARRYING cargo has always been the main job of ships. Even today, in the age of air travel, it is still the cheapest way of transporting goods. In fact, more that 95 per cent of goods are transported around the world in the holds of cargo ships. A cargo ship is basically a long, box-shaped vessel, providing the maximum amount of room inside for cargo. The first cargo ships carried their cargoes in barrels or jars in the hold. Modern cargo ships have been developed to carry specific cargoes, such as oil and cars. There are still many general cargo ships, including container ships. Different types of cargo ship have also been developed for use in rivers, in coastal waters and for long-distance ocean travel. Ocean-going ships are huge and expensive to build, so they are designed to spend as little time as possible in port.

Canal-sized
The Panama Canal in Central America provides an important short-cut for ships travelling between the Atlantic and Pacific oceans. Many cargo ships are built to dimensions called panamax – the largest size that can fit through the canal.

Parts of a container ship
A container is a standard-sized, steel box that can be filled with any sort of cargo. On a container ship, the prepacked containers are stacked in piles in the hold and on the deck. Some of the containers on deck may be refrigerated. The ship is driven by a giant diesel engine.

River barge
A slow, wide barge carries cargo along the river Rhine in Germany. The river reaches from the North Sea deep into the industrial heartland of Germany. Coal, grain and timber are often carried by barges like this one.

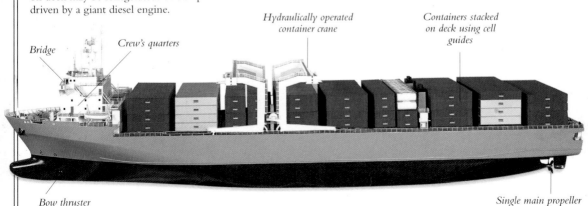

Hydraulically operated container crane

Containers stacked on deck using cell guides

Bridge

Crew's quarters

Bow thruster

Single main propeller

Unloading containers

In port, giant cranes transfer the containers from the ship. The standard-size containers are lowered on to specialized trucks, which carry them to huge dock-side parking lots where they are stacked in rows. The containers are then loaded on to lorries or railway cars and taken to their final destination.

FACT BOX

• The oil tanker *Jahre Viking* is the world's largest ship. It has a deadweight of 564,763 tonnes and is 458m long.

• The world's largest container ship can carry 6,000, 6m-long containers.

• A lighter aboard ship (LASH) carries river barges stacked like containers on its deck. A reefer ship carries fruit and vegetables in its refrigerated holds.

Return to sail

A few cargo ships have experimental computer-controlled sails. The rigid sails are used to save fuel. When set, they move automatically. They are rotated by electric motors guided by computer. Sails like this are very efficient at achieving the best angle to the wind.

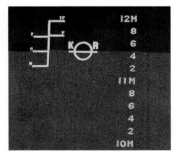

Not too deep

Load lines (also called Plimsoll lines) show how low a ship is safely allowed to float in the water when it is fully loaded. The load lines on the left of the picture are for different types of water. TF means tropical fresh, F is fresh water, T is tropical salt water, S is salt water in summer and W is salt water in winter. The scale on the right shows the distance to the keel of the ship in metres.

Specialist carriers

This ship is specially designed to carry just one sort of cargo – liquefied petroleum gas (LPG), such as methane or butane. The gas must be cooled to a very low temperature to keep it liquid. The pipes on the deck control the gas.

SHIP STABILITY

Many ships look as though they are top heavy, so how do they manage to stay upright and not capsize? These projects will help you find out what makes a ship stable. The shape of the hull's cross-section is important – some hull shapes are more stable than others. When a ship tips over, the hull on that side sinks into the water. On the other side it rises up out of the water. The water creates more upthrust on the side that sinks in, pushing the ship upright again. The more one side of the hull sinks in, the bigger the push and the more stable the hull. The position of the cargo in the hull is important, too. Heavy cargo high up on deck makes the ship top heavy and more likely to tip over. Heavy cargo or equipment low down in the hull makes the ship more stable. Cargo that can move is dangerous, because it could slip to one side of the ship, making it more likely that the ship will tip over. The first project looks at the stability of a multi-hulled boat called a catamaran.

Pile it high
Containers are piled high on the deck of a container ship. The containers are loaded evenly to prevent the ship becoming unstable.

Two hulls
The two hulls of a catamaran are joined together by a strong bridge. This double-hulled shape makes the boat very stable.

MAKE A CATAMARAN

You will need: small plastic bottle, scissors, thin garden cane, elastic bands, some small wooden bricks or other cargo.

1 Remove the top from a small plastic bottle and carefully cut the bottle in half lengthways. This will leave you with two identical shapes to form the catamaran hulls.

2 Place the two halves of the bottle side by side. Lay two medium-length pieces of garden cane on top. Securely fasten the canes to the bottle halves using elastic bands.

3 Put your completed catamaran into a tank or bowl of water. Load the hulls with cargo such as wooden bricks. Can you make your boat capsize?

LOADING CARGO

You will need: plastic bottle and square tub of about the same size, scissors, wooden blocks, modelling clay.

1 For this project you need one container with a round hull shape and another about the same size with a square hull shape. Cut a strip from the round container to make a hold.

2 Put both containers in a tank or bowl of water. Gradually load one side of each hull with wooden blocks. Which hull capsizes first? Which hull is more stable?

3 Now load the square hull evenly with wooden blocks. You should be able to get a lot more in. Press down on one side of the hull. Can you feel the hull trying to right itself?

Unstable round hull
When a round hull tips to one side, there is little change to the amount of hull underwater. This makes the shape unstable.

Stable square hull
When a square hull tips to one side, there is a great change in the amount of hull underwater on that side. This makes it stable.

5 Reload the round hull with wooden blocks. Can you see how the modelling clay ballast low down in the hull has made the craft more stable?

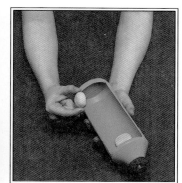

4 To stabilize the round hull, press some lumps of modelling clay into the bottom of the rounded hull. The clay adds weight called ballast to the bottom of the hull.

FERRIES

Cable-drawn ferry
This ferry travels along a chain stretched between the two river banks. Its engine pulls on the chain instead of working a propeller.

ERRIES are ships and boats designed to carry passengers, cars, coaches, trucks and sometimes even trains across water. There are several different types of ferry. Each one is designed for a different type of crossing, such as small, raft-like ferries for short river crossings of a few minutes, or larger cruise-liner ferries for long sea crossings of several days. Most vehicle-carrying ferries have wide doors and ramps at the bow and stern. These allow cars and lorries to quickly drive on and off the ship. They are known as a roll-on, roll-off (or ro-ro) ferry. In a typical large ferry, the lower decks are like a multi-storey car park. The passengers travel on the upper decks, where there are lounges, restaurants and shops. Ferries like this work day and night, all year round. Some ferries, such as catamarans, hydrofoils and hovercraft, are designed for short sea and lake crossings and are much faster.

Loading and unloading
Cars drive along a ramp to reach the car deck of a small ro-ro ferry. The ferry's bow slots into a special dock for the loading process. The ferry will be unloaded through doors at the stern. Larger ferries have separate ramps for loading cars and lorries.

FACT BOX

• The largest superferries have three huge decks to carry up to 850 cars, trucks and coaches. There is room for up to 1,250 passengers in the cabins above.

• Train ferries carry railway coaches and wagons. They have rail tracks on deck that the coaches and wagons roll on to at the docks.

• The world's fastest car ferry is called the *Finnjet* and it operates on the Baltic Sea. It is capable of over 30 knots (55km/h).

Superferry
The huge ferries that travel on long sea routes are called superferries. They can carry hundreds of cars and lorries and thousands of passengers. There are cabins for passengers to sleep in on overnight sailings and shops, restaurants and cinemas to keep people entertained.

Speedy cat

Catamarans like the SeaCat are some of the fastest vehicle-carrying ferries. Having two hulls instead of one and super-powerful, gas turbine engines makes this ferry much faster than a traditional passenger ferry.

Flying in water

A hydrofoil is the fastest type of ferry. Under its hull there are wing-like foils. These lift the hull clear of the water as it speeds along. Lifting the hull out of the water reduces water resistance (drag), allowing the hydrofoil to travel much faster.

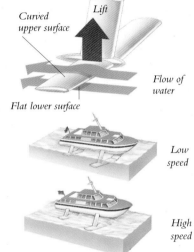

Curved upper surface

Lift

Flow of water

Flat lower surface

Low speed

High speed

How a hovercraft works

A central fan draws in air and forces it between the hull and the skirt. Two large pusher propellers drive the craft along.

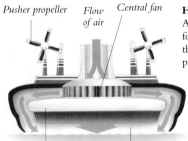

Pusher propeller   *Flow of air*   *Central fan*

Buoyancy tank   *Air cushion*

How a hydrofoil works

Water flows faster over the foil's curved upper surface than it does over the flat lower surface, so creating lift. Foils only work when travelling at high speed. At low speed the boat's hull sits in the water.

Hovering on air

A hovercraft skims across water supported on a cushion of air. The air is held in place by a rubber skirt. A hovercraft can also travel on flat ground, so it can leave the water to load and unload. Buoyancy tanks stop the hovercraft sinking if the air cushion fails.

FISHING BOATS

THERE are millions of fishing boats in the world. Most of them are small traditional boats sailed by a single person or a small crew. Others are larger, commercial fishing boats. The very largest, called factory ships, are able to stay at sea for up to a month. Fishing was one of the earliest uses of boats and dozens of different styles of fishing boat have been developed all over the world. Some fish are caught with hooks and lines or traps, such as pots, left in the sea and attached to the seabed by an anchor. Most fishing, however, is done with nets that trap shoals of fish. Different types of net are used to catch different species of fish. Commercial fishing boats have special equipment for handling the nets and storing the fish they have caught. Many also have sonar equipment for tracking shoals of fish under the water. In the 1970s many countries' fishing industries collapsed due to over-fishing. International regulations now limit the number and size of fish caught in order to preserve fish stocks.

Fishing fleets
Coastal towns and villages all over the world have their own fishing fleets based in small harbours. This one is on the island of Skye in Scotland. Most people in the town are involved in the fishing industry. Laws to reduce catches and conserve fish stocks have hit many small ports.

Inshore fishing boat
This is a typical wooden fishing boat used for fishing in inshore (coastal) waters. It is used up to 100km from port and catches surface-living fish such as herring, mackerel and anchovies.

Deep-sea trawler
Ships designed for fishing hundreds of kilometres off shore have high bows for breaking through waves. Trawlers like this catch fish such as cod, hake and plaice.

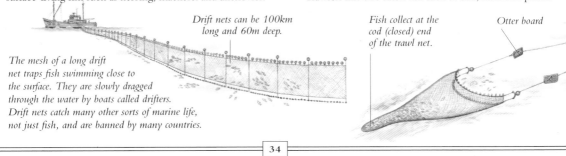

Drift nets can be 100km long and 60m deep.

The mesh of a long drift net traps fish swimming close to the surface. They are slowly dragged through the water by boats called drifters. Drift nets catch many other sorts of marine life, not just fish, and are banned by many countries.

Fish collect at the cod (closed) end of the trawl net.

Otter board

Bringing in the catch

A net bursting with cod and other fish is hauled on board. Fishing nets are pulled in after they have been in the sea for a few hours. A mechanical hoist lifts the full net out of the water. The net's closed end is released and its catch emptied out on deck.

Processing the catch

A catch is sorted as soon as it is on board. The fish may be cleaned and gutted before being frozen. Larger trawlers have equipment on board to process the fish — cutting off heads and tails and removing the bones.

A dip net is used to scoop up fish over the side of the boat.

Traditional fishing

Off the coast of Tanzania, East Africa, many fishermen use outrigger sailboats and dhows. Small fishing boats like these have not changed for many centuries. Nets, lines and spears are used to bring in the catch. Small scale fishing like this does not deplete fish stocks as large commercial vessels can.

Dip net

A stern trawler drags a large trawl net behind it. Ships like this were developed to catch huge shoals of cod living at depths below 15m.

Floats keep the top of the net on the surface.

A shoal near the surface of the sea is quickly encircled by a purse seine net. The net is closed by gathering together the bottom edges like a purse.

Fishing boats and nets

The type of net a boat carries depends on the fish it is going to catch. Some boats fish for species that live near the surface of the sea, while others trawl the waters deeper down. Floats and weights are attached to the net to keep it in shape under the water. For example, otter boards are used to force open the mouth of a trawl. There are regulations restricting the size of the holes in the net so that young fish can escape.

ANCHORS

A N anchor is a device for stopping a ship or boat drifting in the wind or current. It is used when the engines are turned off or the sails taken down. The anchor is attached to the ship by a strong chain and its particular shape makes it catch firm in the seabed. There are several reasons for using an anchor. The most common is for stopping close to shore when there is no harbour or the ship is too big for the harbour (such as an oil tanker). In an emergency, such as an engine failure in bad weather, an anchor can stop a ship drifting on to the shore and being wrecked. Different designs of anchor are suitable for different sizes of ships and for different types of seabed, such as sandy or rocky. The projects on these pages will show you how to make two different types of anchor that are used in very different conditions.

Ship's anchor
This type of anchor is called a stockless anchor and is used on most metal ships. The points of the anchor dig into the seabed, securing the ship.

MAKE A ROCK ANCHOR

You will need: large paper clip, pliers, ruler, short pencil, elastic bands, thin garden cane, scissors, string, tray of pebbles (about 5 to 10cm in size).

Catching the rocks
Your model is similar to an anchor used on a traditional fishing boat. The spikes catch hold of the crevices on a rock-strewn seabed.

1 Unbend a large paper clip using pliers. Cut about 10cm of wire off and bend it slightly. Attach the wire to a short pencil with an elastic band wound tightly round the join.

2 Cut a piece of thin garden cane also about 10cm long. Attach this to the other end of the pencil, but at right angles to the wire. Use an elastic band to secure the cane.

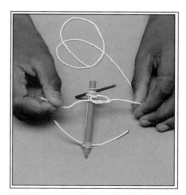

3 Cut a long piece of string for an anchor chain. Tie one end of it to the pencil, below the garden cane. Fill a tray with pebbles to test out your anchor (see opposite).

MAKE A SAND ANCHOR

You will need: large paper clips, pliers, sticky tape, plastic straw, scissors, sheet of plastic, coins, string, tray of sand.

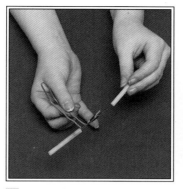

1 Bend a paper clip into a T-shape with a foot. Use pliers to cut another piece of wire to fit across the top of the T. Fix together with tape and two lengths of plastic straw.

2 Cut two blades from a sheet of plastic. Make sure that they will fit inside your T-shape. Tape the blades securely to the upright of the T and the two straws.

3 Find two medium-size coins the same size. Tape one to each blade. The coins add weight to make it dig into the sand better.

Blade

Digging into sand
This is a model of a Danforth anchor. The wide, flat blades dig deep into either a muddy or a sandy seabed.

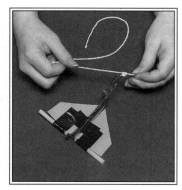

4 Shape another paper clip to make a straight arm with a hook at each end. Hook one end to the anchor and rest the arm in the upright foot. Tie a length of string to the other end. Use a tray of sand to test your anchor.

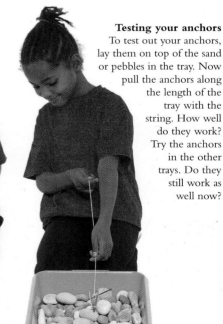

Testing your anchors
To test out your anchors, lay them on top of the sand or pebbles in the tray. Now pull the anchors along the length of the tray with the string. How well do they work? Try the anchors in the other trays. Do they still work as well now?

SAILING

SAILS catch the power of the wind to propel the boat or ship along. Today, sail power is mainly used by leisure craft, for racing and cruising. In some parts of the world, sail power is still common for fishing boats. Sails were originally made of strong cloth called canvas, but are now usually made of synthetic fabrics. Sails are supported by masts and ropes or wires called rigging. Ropes used to trim (adjust) sails are called sheets. Large yachts have different sets of sails for different wind conditions, including small storm sails. There are many different arrangements of masts, sails and rigging. Most modern sailboats and yachts have two triangular sails called a mainsail and jib supported by a single mast. The keel on a yacht and the centreboard on a sailboat stop the boat drifting sideways in the wind. A heavy keel also makes a yacht more stable.

Mainsail · Mainmast · Batten (sail stiffener) · Jib · Boom · Mainsheet · Tiller · Jibsheet · Hull · Rudder · Centreboard

Parts of a sailboat
The main parts of a typical sailboat are shown above. A sailboat like this would usually have a crew of two people – a helmsman who operates the tiller and the mainsail and a crew who works the jib and centreboard. The jib is a small triangular sail in front of the mainmast. Sailboats also use spinnakers (three-cornered sails used in racing) for extra speed.

Racing sailboat
In very windy conditions, the helmsman and crew lean out over the side of the boat. They do this to keep the boat balanced and upright. The crew uses a harness called a trapeze attached to a wire running to the top of the mast. They lean out to the windward side of the boat.

Racing yacht
Large racing yachts have enormous sails and need a large crew to change them quickly. Sails are raised and lowered using winding wheels called winches. Yachts like this are designed to be sailed across oceans.

Cruising yacht

A cruising yacht has comfortable cabins, a galley and bathroom. It has smaller sails than a race yacht and is easier to sail. This type of yacht, rigged with one mast, is known as a sloop. It has two jib sails so it is called cutter rigged.

Old designs

These big, two-masted yachts are called schooners. A schooner has a foremast ahead of the mainmast. Here, their sails are gaff rigged (supporting poles at an angle to the masts).

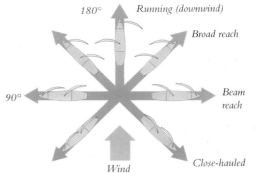

180°   *Running (downwind)*

Broad reach

90°   *Beam reach*

Wind direction   *Close-hauled*

Fastest of all

A trimaran has a main hull and two outriggers. The outriggers make the yacht very stable, which means it can use enormous sails for its size. Although multi-hulled vessels have been in use for centuries, offshore racing trimarans have only been developed since the 1960s. Since then, they have set records for the fastest transatlantic crossing.

Points of sailing

A boat can use the wind to sail in every direction, except straight into the wind. The crew adjust the sails to go in different directions called the points of sailing. To head upwind a boat must follow a zigzag course. This is called tacking. If a boat turns when the wind is behind it, it is known as gybing. Running (sailing downwind) is not the fastest direction. Reaching (sailing across the wind) is faster.

FACT BOX

• The first person to sail solo around the world was an American called Joshua Slocum. The voyage took three years and Slocum could not swim.

• The record time for sailing around the world is 74 days, 22 hours and 17 minutes. It was set in 1994 by the catamaran *Enza*.

• In the galley (kitchen) of a yacht, the cooker is mounted on hinges. This keeps it level when the boat heels over in the wind.

SAILS FOR POWER

T HE project on these pages will show you how to make a model of a simple sailboat. Once you have made your model, use it to find out how a sailing boat works and how sailors use the wind. To sail in the direction the sailor wants to go, he or she must look at the direction that the wind is blowing from and adjust the position of the sails to make the most use of the wind. A boat can sail in every direction except straight into the wind. When a boat faces directly into the wind, its sails flap uselessly and the boat is in the no-go zone. To sail towards a place where the wind is blowing from, the sailors must sail a zigzag course. This means first sailing across the wind one way, then sailing across it the other. This is called tacking. Making the most of the wind is the art of sailing and it takes lots of practice. Sailors have to learn to control many different parts of the boat at the same time.

Finished boat
Once you have finished your boat, you could try adding a centreboard. Does it make any difference to the boat's handling?

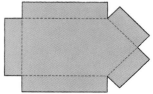

MAKE A SAILBOAT

You will need: pencil, ruler, thick card, scissors, sticky tape, plastic sheet, stapler, bradawl, modelling clay, thin garden canes, coloured paper, plastic straws, small plastic bottle, string, paper clip.

Template
Use this template to make your model. The dimensions are 25cm by 10cm, with sides about 4cm deep.

1 Cut out your hull shape from thick card, using the template above as a guide. Score along the broken lines with the scissors. Use sticky tape to fix the sides together.

2 Lay the hull on a plastic sheet. Cut around it leaving a 5cm gap around it to overlap the sides. Fold the plastic over the sides of the hull and staple it in place.

3 Pierce a hole in the middle of a strip of card a little wider than the hull. Staple in place. Put modelling clay under the hole. Push a 30cm cane through the hole into the clay.

4 Cut a sail from paper. Attach a straw along the side and a garden cane along the bottom with sticky tape. Slip the straw over the mast.

5 Cut an L-shape (about 8cm long, 4cm wide at base and 2cm wide at top) from the small plastic bottle. Cut the base of the L in half to make two tabs, as shown.

6 Fold back the L-shape's two tabs in opposite directions and staple them to the stern (back) of the boat. This is the boat's rudder.

Finding out about the points of sailing

When you test your boat out, try setting the sails in these different positions. Alter the position of the sail by using the string taped to the boom (cane). Follow the arrows shown here to see which way the wind should be blowing from in each case. Why not try blowing from other directions to see if this makes a difference to your boat?

Direction of wind

8 To test out how your sail boat works, make a breeze by waving a large sheet of paper near to the boat. Adjust the string to move the sail in to the right position.

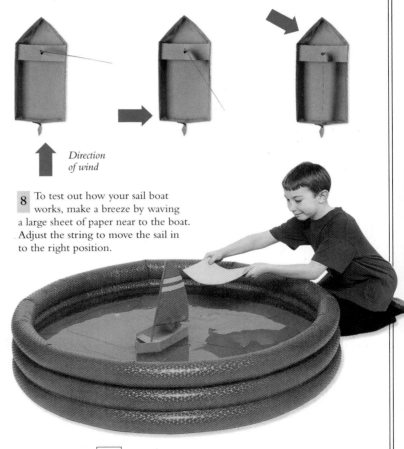

7 Cut a piece of string about 20cm long. Tape one end to the back of the boom (the cane) and feed the other end through a paper clip attached to the back of the boat.

WARSHIPS

THE first true warships were the many-oared galleys of ancient Greece and Rome. By the 1400s, heavily-armed galleons with many cannons were developed. In the early 1900s, steam-driven, iron battleships were the forerunners of modern warships. Today's warships carry a huge amount of special equipment. They have weapons for attacking other ships and submarines, weapons for defending themselves against air attack, and electronic equipment for tracking ships and aircraft and controlling their weapons. The largest warships are aircraft carriers, which act as air bases at sea. Smaller warships, such as frigates and destroyers, are designed for speed and have powerful gas turbine engines. The smallest ships are minesweepers and patrol boats. A country's navy defends its waters, transports and supports fighting troops and helps in emergencies around the world. A navy needs many ships to keep its warships supplied with fuel, food and ammunition.

Operations room
At the heart of a warship is the operations room. From here the crew monitor what other ships and aircraft are doing and make decisions about what actions to take.

Frigate
A frigate is a small, fast-moving ship used to escort convoys of larger ships. It carries anti-submarine and anti-aircraft weapons. Small frigates are sometimes called corvettes.

FACT BOX

• Aircraft carriers are the largest warships. They have displacements of more than 90,000 tonnes and crews of 5,000 sailors and air crew.

• During World War I (1914–18) huge battleships fought at sea. Their weapons were enormous guns. Hulls were protected by 40cm-thick armour.

• The world's largest submarines are Russian Typhoon class. They have displacements of 26,500 tonnes and are 170m long.

Destroyer
A destroyer is generally larger than a frigate and is an all-purpose warship. This guided-missile destroyer has several radar dishes for weapons control as well as navigation. It also has a helicopter deck at the stern.

Helicopter
deck

Anti-aircraft
missile launcher

Radars and
communication
aerials

Funnel

Gun turret

Rocket
launcher

Bridge

Anti-aircraft
missile launcher

Exocet
missile
launcher

Parts of a warship

This is an overhead view of
a frigate. You can clearly see
the sharp bows and narrow hull
that help to give it speed. It has a
range of guns and missiles aboard
ship as well as armed helicopters.

Naval guns

Modern naval
guns, such as this
114mm single
gun, are aimed
automatically. A
fire-control radar
keeps track of the
target and moves
the gun from side
to side and up and
down. Missiles are
also used to bring
down enemy
aircraft. Some
have on-board
sensors that home
in on their target.

Airfield at sea

An aircraft carrier's deck is a runway where aircraft take off and land.
The runway is short so a steam catapult is used to help launch the
aircraft at take-off. Underneath the deck is a
hangar where aircraft are stored and serviced.
The aircrafts' wings fold up to save
storage space below deck.

Support ships

This ship is a specialized support ship used in
landing troops. In the stern is a dock for landing
craft to be loaded. The landing craft ferry troops
and equipment to the shore.

Inflatables

Special forces, such as commandos, use small,
fast inflatable craft for transferring from ship
to shore. This boat can be used above the water
or underwater as a diving craft. It can even be
submerged and hidden on the seabed until it is
needed. You can see the electrically
powered propeller for underwater use.

*Inflatable dinghy (small
boat) is powered by two
outboard motors.*

SUBMARINES

A submarine is a vessel that can travel submerged under the water as well as on the water's surface. Most submarines are naval ships. There are two main types – hunter-killer, or patrol submarines, which search for and try to sink enemy shipping, and ballistic missile submarines, which carry nuclear missiles. Naval submarines use two different types of power – conventional and nuclear. When a conventional submarine is on the surface its diesel engine makes electricity. The electricity is used to run the electric motors that work the propeller and also to recharge the batteries. When the submarine is submerged, the diesel engine is turned off and the electric motor is powered by the batteries. In a nuclear submarine, the power comes from a nuclear reactor. The main weapon of a hunter-killer submarine is the torpedo – a sort of underwater missile. Another type of underwater vessel is the submersible. Submersibles are small diving craft used for ocean research, exploration and the repair of undersea pipes and cables.

View of outside

View of inside

The Turtle
American engineer David Bushnell built the first working submarine in 1775. It was called the *Turtle* and made of wood. It was moved by two screw-shaped, hand-operated propellers.

Nuclear submarine
A nuclear submarine, such as this Trident, can stay submerged for months on end. Its reactor can run for this long without refuelling. An air conditioning plant recycles the air on board to make fresh air.

U-boat
The potential of the submarine as a weapon was realised during World War II (1939–45). The German U-boats (*Unterseeboot*) had greatly increased range and speed. They sank thousands of Allied ships with their torpedoes.

Parts of a submarine

A modern submarine, such as this nuclear ballistic missile submarine, is nearly as long as a football pitch – around 91m. It has a crew of around 140 who work in shifts. Like other ships, it has an engine, propeller and rudder at the stern. Heat from the nuclear reactor generates steam. This drives the turbines that turn the submarine's propeller. Like all submarines, its hull is strong, but very few submarines can go below 500m. Buoyancy tanks fill with water to submerge the submarine. To resurface, compressed air pushes the water out of the tanks. Small movable wings, called hydroplanes, control the submarine's direction.

Towers and periscopes

The conning tower stands clear of the water when a submarine surfaces. Communication masts and periscopes top the tower. Periscopes are a device that allows the crew to see above water when the submarine is submerged. There are usually two periscopes – a large one for general observation and a smaller one for attack.

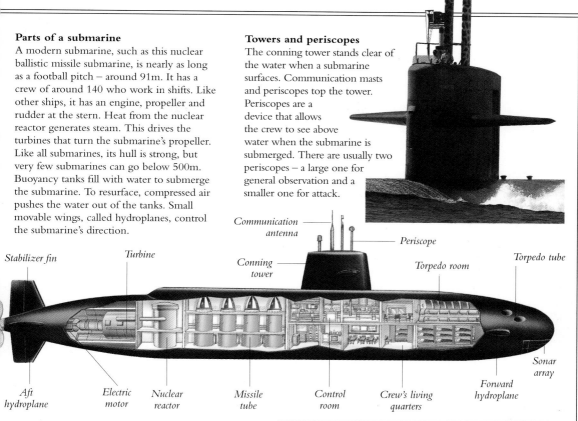

Stabilizer fin

Turbine

Communication antenna

Periscope

Conning tower

Torpedo room

Torpedo tube

Aft hydroplane

Electric motor

Nuclear reactor

Missile tube

Control room

Crew's living quarters

Forward hydroplane

Sonar array

Mini-submersible

Small submersibles, carrying one or two people, are used to work at depths that would be too dangerous for a free-swimming diver. They are equipped with cameras, floodlights and robot arms. Highly accurate navigation systems allow the crew to find their way in the pitch black of the seabed. A mini-submersible runs on batteries and can stay under only for a short time – less than a day.

Research submersible

Teams of people dive to the ocean floor in submersibles. They have extremely strong hulls for diving very deep, up to about 8km. Submersibles dive and return to a support ship waiting on the surface. Special, deep-diving vessels called bathyscaphes can dive even farther – up to 11km.

DIVING AND SURFACING

A submarine dives by making itself heavier so that it sinks. It surfaces again by making itself lighter. To do this, it uses large tanks called buoyancy tanks. When the submarine is on the surface, the buoyancy tanks are full of air. To make the submarine dive, the tanks are flooded with seawater, making the submarine heavy enough to sink. To make the submarine surface again, compressed air is pumped into the tanks, forcing the water out. This makes the submarine lighter and it floats to the surface. In this project, you can make a model submarine that can dive and surface using buoyancy tanks. When it is underwater, a full-scale submarine moves up and down using hydroplanes. These are like tiny wings and work like rudders as the submarine moves along. Submarines need very strong hulls to prevent them from being crushed by the huge pressure under the water. As submarines dive down, the weight of the water pressing down on them becomes greater and greater. The tremendous pressure from the water builds up quickly.

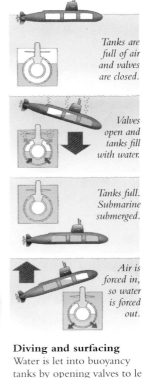

Tanks are full of air and valves are closed.

Valves open and tanks fill with water.

Tanks full. Submarine submerged.

Air is forced in, so water is forced out.

MAKE A SUBMARINE

You will need: large plastic bottle, sand, plastic funnel, two small plastic bottles, bradawl, scissors, ruler, two plastic drinking straws, elastic bands, modelling clay, two small bulldog clips.

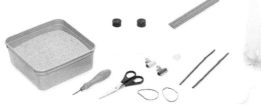

Diving and surfacing
Water is let into buoyancy tanks by opening valves to let the air out. Water is expelled by pumping in air stored in tanks of compressed air.

1 Fill the large plastic bottle with sand using a funnel. Fill it until it just sinks in a tank of water. Test out the bottle (cap firmly screwed on) to find the right amount of sand.

2 Make a large hole (about 1cm across) in one side of two small plastic bottles. On the other side make a small hole, big enough for a plastic straw to fit into.

3 Attach the two small bottles to either side of the large bottle using elastic bands. Twist the small bottles so that the small hole on each one points upwards.

4 Push a plastic drinking straw into each small hole so that a bit pokes through. Seal around the base of the straws with modelling clay to make a watertight join.

5 Put a small bulldog clip about halfway down each straw. The clips need to be strong enough to squash the straw and stop air being forced out by the water.

6 Put your model submarine in a tank of water. With the clips on it should float. Remove the clips and water will flood the buoyancy tanks. The submarine will sink.

Final adjustments
This is the finished model submarine. You might find your model sinks bow first, or stern first. If this is the case, level it by shaking the sand evenly inside the bottle.

8 When your model submarine has resurfaced, keep blowing slowly into the tanks. Replace each bulldog clip and your model submarine will remain floating on the surface.

7 To make the submarine surface again, blow slowly into both straws at once. The air will force the water out of the buoyancy tanks and the submarine will rise to the surface.

PLEASURE CRAFT

THERE are many boats and ships designed for relaxation and sport. Boats offer a huge range of activities, from hiring a rowing boat to cruising the oceans in a luxury yacht. Many people enjoy cruising and touring holidays afloat. Some holidaymakers operate the boat themselves, while others take the opportunity to relax with a crew to do the sailing. The ocean liners that regularly sailed across the world's seas have long gone, but their place has been taken by cruise liners. These ships are like floating hotels and are specifically designed for holidaymakers. On holiday, a cruise ship usually calls at a number of different ports. Some enthusiasts even sail right around the world. Watersports such as rowing, canoeing, sailing and windsurfing are very popular. Spectacular tricks and stunts can be executed on windsurfers, surfboards and body boards. Canoes and kayaks offer the excitement of shooting down white-water rapids. Other people enjoy racing in sailboats, yachts, rowing boats and powerboats.

Wind and waves
In strong winds a windsurfer can perform amazing flying leaps using a funboard. The surfboard is steered by a sail. Experienced surfers take part in competitions, such as course racing and wave performance.

White-water racing
A kayak has a closed cockpit so that no water can get into the hull, even in very rough water. This makes it excellent for white-water racing. There are two types of racing. In wildwater racing, canoeists are timed over a course of obstacles such as rocks and rapids. In slalom, canoeists negotiate a course of gates.

Touring canoe
The canoe is an open boat, as opposed to the closed cockpit of a kayak. The canoeist sits or kneels and can use either single or double-bladed paddles. Canadian canoes are used for slalom races over a set course. Open canoes are a good way of seeing the natural world, because they move quietly through the water, not disturbing the peace.

Rafting

Travelling down the turbulent waters of a mountain river in an inflatable raft is a popular adventure sport. Rafters use single-bladed paddles. Everybody wears a lifejacket because there is a danger of falling out of the raft.

Sailing cruiser

Many people enjoy days out and longer holidays on sailing cruisers. This yacht, the *Wind Spirit*, is a cross between a sailing yacht and a cruise liner.

Luxury cruiser

A few people are lucky enough to be able to afford a large luxury motor yacht, or cruiser, like this. These yachts are equipped with every sort of luxury as well as the latest in satellite navigation equipment and cruise control.

Powerboat racing

A ride in a powerboat is incredibly fast, but very bumpy. Their hulls are specially shaped to skim across the surface. There are two types of powerboat racing – inshore and offshore. Boats are put into different classes, depending on their size and engine. Fast Formula 1 powerboats race all over the world.

Cruise liner

Many people spend their holidays on cruise liners. The liners travel around scenic parts of the world, stopping at interesting ports. A large cruise liner is part resort and part luxury hotel. It may be equipped with swimming pool, whirlpool, sundecks, tennis courts, gym, theatre and even a golf course.

SERVICE BOATS

SERVICE vessels do special jobs in rivers or at sea, usually to help other boats and ships. The most common service boat is the tug. The tug's main job is to move other ships, sometimes to manoeuvre them into harbour, other times because their engines have failed. The largest tugs, called salvage tugs, can tow even the biggest cargo ships, and also help in emergency situations. Tugs have high bows to break through large waves, a high bridge to give a good view, a large deck to carry cargo and on-board winches. They also have extremely powerful engines and are highly manoeuvrable. A selection of service vessels is shown here. There are many more, however, such as cable-laying ships, oil drilling vessels and light ships. Lifeboats are also service boats.

Towing to sea
These tugs are towing part of an oil rig. They will tow it all the way from where is was built to its station at sea. Each tug has a strong towing hook where two steel ropes are attached.

Dredger
A dredger digs silt (mud and particles carried by water) from the bottom of rivers and canals. It does this to stop them becoming too shallow. A bucket dredger is shown below. It uses a long line of buckets to scoop silt into a barge.

Research ship
An ocean research ship is a floating science laboratory. This ship has a bathymetry system for surveying the seabed. It also has on-board computer systems and equipment for lowering instruments and submersibles into the sea. It can carry 18 marine and technical staff on voyages of over 40 days. The engines have been specially modified to reduce engine noise, which might affect sensitive recordings. Research vessels like this help biologists to explore life on the seabed. They also help oceanographers (scientists who study the oceans) to examine undersea mountains and trenches.

Two tugs manoeuvre the bow.

Supertanker

Two tugs push the stern.

The tugs push on opposite sides to turn the ship around.

Pushing around

These tugs are manoeuvring a huge supertanker into port. The tanker is so big it has difficulty steering in enclosed waters. Tugs using towlines and pushing with their bows can turn the ship around. They gently nudge it into its berth or to an offshore mooring buoy.

Fire fighting

Every major port has a fire-fighting tug on stand-by all the time. It sprays foam or water, which is sucked from the sea by powerful pumps. The water is fired from guns on the upper deck on to burning ships or port buildings. Foam is used to smother oil and chemical fires from tankers.

Floating crane

A salvage barge is like a floating crane. It is used to recover sunken or capsized vessels. Huge cranes like this can lift large cargo ships from the seabed.

Breaking the ice

An icebreaker has a very strong hull. It is designed to ride up on the ice so that the ship's weight breaks through the thick ice. Most icebreakers have propellers in the bow to draw the smashed ice back behind the ship. Some also have special tanks on board to allow the ship to heel over if necessary to free it from the surrounding ice. Icebreakers are used to keep shipping lanes in northern waters open during winter. They are used in countries such as Canada, Denmark, Russia, Sweden and the USA.

NAVIGATION AND SIGNALLING

One

Two

Three

C (yes)

N (no)

O (man overboard)

G (I require a pilot)

AT sea, navigation includes many different jobs. It involves planning a safe route, checking the ship's position regularly to see how it is progressing, avoiding collisions with other vessels, and keeping an eye on the weather. The basic tools of navigation are a chart (map) of the sea and a magnetic compass. The chart shows coastlines, the depth of the water, landmarks on shore, hazards such as wrecks, the strength of tides and so on. Modern navigating tools, such as satellite-controlled Global Positioning System (GPS), mean that boats and ships with the correct equipment always know their position. Lighthouses and buoys help with navigation by indicating safe shipping channels and hazards. Signals are a way of sending messages to the shore or another vessel without using radio. Ways of signalling include signal flags and lamps.

Signal flags

An international system of signal flags has been used for centuries. Each flag stands for a number, a letter or a complete message. A flag's basic meaning can be changed by hoisting it on a different mast or in a certain combination with other flags. A selection of flags, with their meanings, is shown here.

A light at sea

A lighthouse warns of dangerous islands, rocks and headlands. It sends out a bright beam of light that sweeps round in a circle. At sea, it appears as a flashing light. Anchored light ships are also used to mark treacherous spots.

Signal lamp

Morse code (a code of long and short pulses) is another way of sending messages. An Aldis lamp has a trigger that the operator uses to turn the light on and off.

Aldis lamp

Lantern

When lighthouses needed people to run them, the crew's quarters were in the tower. Today, most are on automatic.

Compass rose

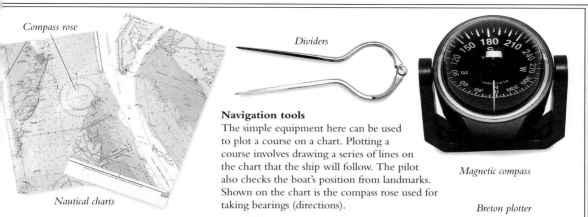

Nautical charts

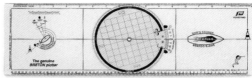

Dividers

Magnetic compass

Navigation tools

The simple equipment here can be used to plot a course on a chart. Plotting a course involves drawing a series of lines on the chart that the ship will follow. The pilot also checks the boat's position from landmarks. Shown on the chart is the compass rose used for taking bearings (directions).

Breton plotter

Parallel ruler

Navigation buoys

The shape and colour of a buoy give it its meaning. Most buoys are red or green and indicate the sides of a safe channel. All buoys have flashing lights as well.

A red port buoy marks the lefthand side of a channel.

A green starboard buoy marks the righthand side of a channel.

Yellow and black cardinal buoys mark hazards or points of interest.

Electronic navigation

The navigation equipment on a modern ship includes radar, sonar and satellite receivers. Radar shows the position of the coast and other ships. Sonar shows the depth of water under the ship. Satellite GPS gives the ship's exact position to within a few metres.

Computers in navigation

At the chart table of this yacht are several computers. One receives images directly from a weather satellite. Another displays the ship's position on an electronic chart.

NAVIGATION LIGHTS

THERE are no street lights at sea, so all vessels have to display lights to warn other vessels that they are there. The types of light and number of them depend on the size of the vessel and what it is doing. For example, a sailboat must carry a white light at the top of its mast. A small powered boat that is underway must carry a red/green light and a white light above it. A red light is always hung on the port side (the lefthand side as you face the bow) of a boat or ship, while a green light is hung on the starboard (right). The project on these pages will show you how to make a simple red/green light. Larger ships that are underway carry a red/green light and several white lights. From these lights, the crew of one ship can tell what size another ship is, whether it is moving and which direction it is going in. This is especially important at night or in fog when visibility is poor. Fishing boats also display extra coloured lights when they are fishing so that other ships can avoid their nets.

Moving to starboard (right).

Moving to port (left).

Heading straight ahead.

MAKE A NAVIGATION LIGHT

You will need: pencil, ruler, thick card, scissors, four insulated wires, screwdriver, two bulb holders and bulbs, modelling clay, sticky tape, clear plastic bottle, red and green coloured plastic, battery.

Which way?
The colour of the light you can see shows which way the ship is moving.

1 Draw out a simple boat shape about 30cm long and 20cm wide on a sheet of thick card. Give the shape a pointed bow and a flat stern. Cut out your shape.

2 Attach two wires to a bulb holder, one either side. Screw in a bulb. Fix the holder to the centre of your boat shape with a piece of modelling clay.

3 Cut three rectangles of card, about 10cm by 6cm. Trim one corner of each piece of card to fit around the bulb and holder. When fixed they will divide up the light.

4 Fix the trimmed ends of the three pieces of card together. Fit over the bulb and stick to the boat base.

5 Cut two rectangles of plastic from a bottle. Tape green transparent plastic to one and red to the other.

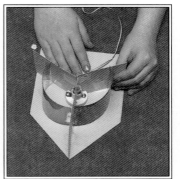

6 Tape the red plastic to the left (port) side of the boat. Tape the green to the right (starboard) side.

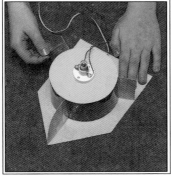

7 Cut a circle of card and tape it over the bulb and coloured windows to make a lid. Fix another bulb and bulb holder with wires attached to the top of the boat.

9 Try testing out your red/green light in a darkened room. Ask a friend to observe while you walk towards him or her. Can they tell which way the boat is moving? Is it coming towards them, away from them, to their left, or to their right?

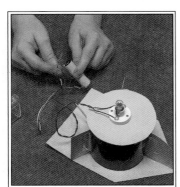

8 Now attach a battery. Tape a wire from each bulb to one end of the battery. Tape the other two wires to the other end of the battery. Both bulbs should light up.

SHIPPING DISASTERS

THE seas and oceans can be very dangerous places. Every year, hundreds of ships are lost and many of their crews drown. The worst hazard is the weather. Strong winds blowing across a wide expanse of water create huge waves as tall as a house. The waves can swamp a small boat or cause a ship to capsize. Long, high waves can break the back of a ship if they lift its bow and stern, leaving its centre unsupported. Another main cause of accidents is human error. Mistakes in communication or navigation cause collisions between vessels, perhaps sinking one of them. Ships also run aground due to errors in navigation. Other accidents are caused by engine failures, fires or explosions. These can have very serious consequences if a ship is carrying a dangerous cargo that may cause long-lasting damage to the environment.

Running aground
Once a ship has run aground it is hard to refloat. If it runs aground on rocks it may even be holed. Eventually a wreck like this will break up in the waves.

Fire on board
Despite being surrounded by water, fire is one of the worst hazards at sea. This ship is lucky that there is a fire boat in range. Usually the crew have to fight the fire themselves.

FACT BOX

• At sea, distances are measured in nautical miles. One nautical mile equals 1,852m. Speed is measured in knots. One knot equals one nautical mile per hour.

• Depth was once measured in fathoms. One fathom was 6ft, which equals 1.83m.

• The biggest collision at sea was between two oil tankers. Their combined deadweight was 660,000 tonnes. Around 300,000 tonnes of oil were spilt into the Caribbean Sea.

Tanker disaster
The oil tanker *MV Braer* ran aground in the Shetland Islands, Scotland, in 1993. The hull was holed and 80,000 tonnes of oil leaked into the sea, creating a huge oil slick. Spills like this result in major ecological damage.

Deadly oil
Seabirds caught in an oil slick are most at risk. They try to clean their feathers and swallow the harmful oil. If birds are caught in time, they can be cleaned with detergents.

Beach clean up
If an oil slick reaches the shore, it coats the rocks with oily sludge. Clearing up a large spill with suction pumps takes months and is very expensive. The coastline takes years to recover.

Capsize
Once a boat has capsized it is almost impossible to right again. The crew may survive by climbing inside the hull or sitting on top of it. Even the largest ships can capsize if they are hit by a very large, rogue wave.

The sinking of the *Titanic*
The most famous shipping disaster of all was the sinking of the ocean liner *Titanic* on April 15, 1912. With the loss of 1,517 lives it remains one of the worst peacetime disasters. This painting of the event is exaggerated – the ship's hull was holed by ice under the water. The disaster was made worse because there were not enough lifeboats.

IN AN EMERGENCY

Lifeboat stations
In an emergency, passengers on this cruise liner would get in the lifeboats shown here. The lifeboats would be lowered down the side of the ship, into the sea.

WHEN an accident does happen, the crew immediately begin to follow an emergency procedure. If they have a radio, they will send a May Day call to the emergency services. Other vessels in the area will go to help, a lifeboat may be launched, or a helicopter sent to search. To help rescuers locate their stricken vessel, flares are fired and emergency horns sounded. Larger boats and ships have an automatic radio beacon that sends out a distress call when it falls into the sea. The emergency services can home in on the beacon. If the crew have to abandon ship, they put on life jackets, perhaps survival suits, and launch lifeboats or life rafts. All but the smallest vessels have fire-fighting equipment on board. A cruise liner will have a computerized warning and sprinkler system.

FACT BOX

• Ships on which there is a risk of explosion, such as drilling and gas-carrying ships, have lifeboats next to the crew compartments. These drop into the sea for quick evacuation.

• If a submarine cannot surface, its crew escape in buoyant personal escape suits. These act as life rafts on the surface.

• The crew of an offshore lifeboat wear helmets and are harnessed to their seats to stop them flying about as waves crash into the boat.

Inshore lifeboats
Small lifeboats, such as this Australian surfboat, help to rescue people near the coast. Swimmers, surfers and sailboat users are rescued quickly by boats like this. It is specially designed to ride over the high surf.

Lifeboat launch
Offshore lifeboats can be swiftly launched down a slipway. When the emergency call comes through, the crew jump into the boat, start the engine and release a holding wire. The boat hits the water at speed. This is a much faster way to launch a boat than setting off from a harbour.

Life rafts

Inflatable life rafts are stored in a container on the deck of a ship or yacht. When the container is thrown into the sea, the raft inflates automatically. It is designed to maintain body heat and not capsize. Inside the raft are medical and food supplies.

Lifeboat at sea

Offshore lifeboats are designed to operate in the worst weather at sea. They have very powerful engines for reaching an emergency quickly. Lifeboats are self-righting and quickly come upright if a wave knocks them flat.

Helicopter rescue

A helicopter winchman is lowered on to a lifeboat. He carries a cradle to pick up a casualty from the boat. Air-sea rescue helicopters take part in searches, winch crew from stricken ships and carry casualties quickly to hospitals on shore.

Foghorn

Flares

The coastguard

Some countries have coastal patrol boats. This Canadian patrol boat is operated by the coastguard service. It acts as a police boat as well as a lifeboat.

Flares and horns

Sailors in trouble fire flares and sound foghorns to show up their position. Flares are like large fireworks. Some simply burn brightly. Others fire a burning light into the sky. The foghorn uses compressed air to make an ear-piercing noise.

KEEPING AFLOAT

MAKE A
SELF-RIGHTING BOAT

You will need: pencil, ruler, polystyrene tile, scissors, modelling clay, elastic bands, small plastic tub.

A crew's first reaction in a collision or grounding is to try to keep their ship afloat if possible. For a start, all ships have bilge pumps. These are used to pump water out of the bottom of the boat's hull and into the sea. Small boats, such as sailboats and canoes, have bags of air or blocks of polystyrene inside to keep them afloat. Most lifeboats are self-righting, which means that they bob back upright if they capsize. Lifeboats are built of tough, lightweight materials such as plastic and foam. They are completely watertight – even their air inlets have seals to keep out the water. Their heavy engines are set low down, while the hull and high-up cabins are full of air. This arrangement ensures that the lifeboat flips upright without needing help. You can find out how to make a simple self-righting boat in the first project.

The hull of a large ship below the waterline is divided into watertight sections by strong metal walls called bulkheads. The doors in the bulkheads are also watertight when they are closed. These are designed so that if one section floods, the water cannot fill the whole hull. Even if a ship is sinking, bulkheads stop it from capsizing due to water rushing to one side. In the second project you can test out how a hull with bulkheads works much better than one without bulkheads.

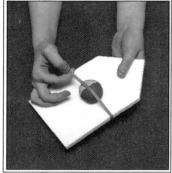

1 Cut a boat-shape about 15cm by 10cm from polystyrene. Attach a golf-ball size lump of modelling clay to one side with an elastic band.

2 Put your boat into a tank or bowl of water. Have the modelling clay, which represents the crew and equipment, on top. If you capsize the boat it will stay capsized.

3 Add another lump of modelling clay underneath the boat to represent heavy engines or ballast. Add an upturned plastic tub on top to represent a watertight cabin.

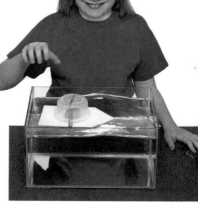

4 Now try to capsize it again and it will flip back upright. This is because air trapped underwater by the tub and a heavy weight on top forces the boat upright again.

INSTALLING BULKHEADS

You will need: plastic container and lid, bradawl, marbles, scissors, modelling clay, wooden blocks or other cargo.

1 Pierce a hole in one corner of a plastic container using a bradawl. This represents the holed hull of a cargo ship.

2 Add some marbles (cargo) and lower the container into a tank of water. It will fill up with water and slowly sink.

3 Cut three rectangles from the lid of the container. Make sure they fit across the tub. Round off the bottom corners if you need to.

5 Put some cargo in each section of the hull and put the whole thing back into the water. This time the container will stay afloat because only one section floods. The bulkheads prevent the water filling the whole hull.

Sinking feeling
Find out how many sections need to be holed before the container will sink.

4 Position the plastic walls inside the container so that they divide it into four compartments. Press modelling clay around the edges to make a watertight seal.

IN PORT

Ships and boats move cargo and people from place to place, so they need ports where they can load and unload. Every port has areas called docks where ships tie up along the quayside. The docks are often inside an area of water called a harbour, which is protected from the sea by a massive stone wall or natural cliffs. On the dock are huge cranes for unloading the ships and warehouses for storing cargo. In the port area there may be ship repair yards, parts shops and customs offices. Until recently, large numbers of people were employed as dockers and many major coastal towns and cities have grown up around ports. But the increased use of containers has dramatically reduced the number of workers. Huge merchant ships now dock at purpose-built ports or terminals, which are specially designed for handling cargoes, such as containers, oil and gas.

Tying up
Berthing ropes hooked over bollards are used to tie ships to the quayside. Quays may also be known as wharves.

Container port
An aerial view shows part of Hong Kong's vast container terminal. Special loading cranes, called straddle carriers, are used to fetch and carry the containers.

The pilot
The entrance to a harbour is often narrow and busy. It may also have treacherous shallow areas such as sandbanks outside it. A pilot is a person who knows the harbour well. He or she always takes control of large ships to guide them as they enter and leave the port.

Marina

A marina is a small harbour area where leisure craft such as motorboats and sailing yachts tie up. Marinas are usually separate from the normal harbour. They are also common on coasts where there are few natural harbours for small boats to shelter in. Each bay, called a berth, in a marina has water and electricity supplies.

High and dry

Repair and maintenance facilities in port may include a dry dock. This submarine is being repaired in dry dock. The submarine entered the dock when it was flooded with water. The gates were then closed and the water pumped out. Scaffolding is erected to keep the submarine upright.

Unloading in port

A dockside crane unloads a Japanese ship in the port of Vladivostock, Russia. The crane can be moved along the dockside on railway tracks. This ship's decks, as well as its hold, are piled with freight packed in boxes called tea chests.

Old harbours

The old harbour at Sydney, Australia, is a popular tourist attraction. Many old docks are too small for modern merchant ships. After years of neglect, their harbours are being renovated to provide leisure facilities.

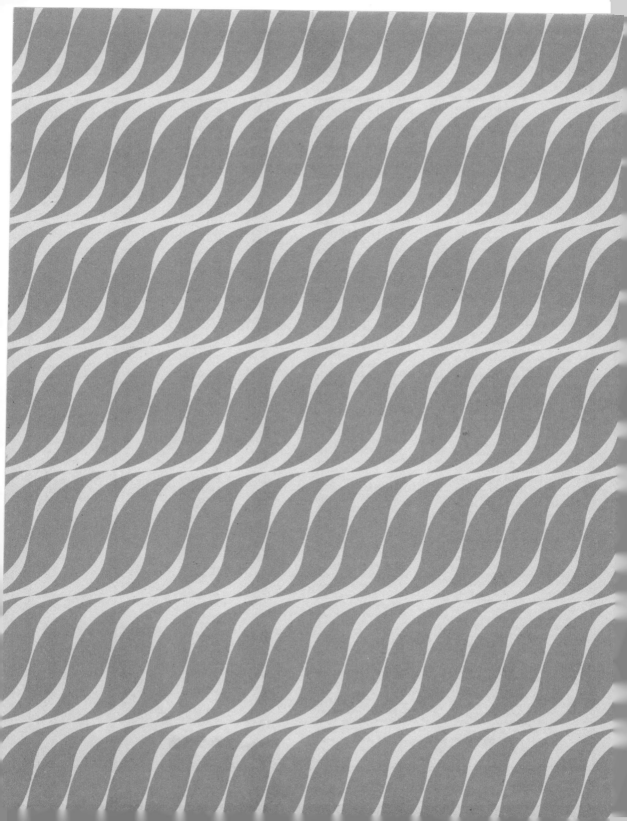